THE HADRIAN'S WALL TRAIL

PHOTOGRAPHY
GRAEME PEACOCK

TEXT
PAUL FRODSHAM

NORTHERN
HERITAGE

Northern Heritage,
Units 7&8 New Kennels, Blagdon Estate, Seaton Burn,
Newcastle upon Tyne NE13 6DB
Telephone: 01670 789 940
www.northern-heritage.co.uk

ISBN No.978-0-9544777-8-3

Printed and bound in China by 1010 Printing International Limited.

British Library Cataloguing in Publishing Data
A catalogue record for this book is available from the British Library.

Places featured in this book are managed and interpreted for the public
by a combination of agencies including English Heritage, the National
Trust, local authorities, conservation charities and private landowners.
When visiting them, please treat them with respect and avoid damaging
ancient monuments (eg by climbing on walls) or disturbing natural
habitats. Details of opening times, admission charges etc are available from
tourist information centres.

GRAEME PEACOCK

Graeme Peacock is one of the best known and
highly regarded photographers of landscapes and
architecture in the North of England. A former Town
Planner, born 'n bred on Tyneside, Graeme has for
over 20 years built up a stock in excess of 49,000
stunning colour images of our region. Regular
clients include The National Trust, English Heritage,
Ordnance Survey and The Royal Mail. To see more
Graeme Peacock images visit his website
www.graeme-peacock.com

INTRODUCTION

Hadrian's Wall, one of the best-known ancient monuments in the world, was built by order of the emperor Hadrian in the years following his visit to Britain in AD122. It is usually thought to have been built to defend the northern boundary of the Roman Empire, but exactly why it was built is not known for sure. There are suggestions that northern British tribes were actively campaigning against Rome at the time of Hadrian's visit, but the Wall seems an extraordinary over-reaction to any such threat. Hadrian wished to stabilise the fringes of the Empire rather than conquer further territory, and frontier defence systems were also constructed along its eastern and southern boundaries. However, these did not approach Hadrian's Wall in terms of architectural sophistication. It may well be that Hadrian, who fancied himself as an architect, drew up the original plans for the Wall himself, and its grand form may conceivably owe as much to his desire to construct great monuments as to any pressing military requirement.

Invariably regarded as a monument to the power and prestige of the mighty Roman Empire, the Wall may also be viewed, quite legitimately, as a monument to failure: if the Romans had succeeded in conquering Scotland, which they tried and failed to do, then no-one would ever have contemplated building a wall for 80 Roman miles (117km) from coast to coast across the wilds of central Britain. Regardless of this, once built, the Wall complex was garrisoned and maintained by Rome for three centuries before its eventual abandonment in the early 5th century.

The Wall, originally about fifteen feet high, had a small fortlet, known to us as a milecastle, every Roman mile along its length, and two turrets spaced equidistantly in each gap between the milecastles. A great defensive ditch ran to the north of the Wall, parallel to it, and another ditch known as the vallum ran to its south, possibly to demarcate the southern edge of a military zone running the length of the Wall. The great Wall forts such as Housesteads were not part of the original plan, but seem to have been added as part of a major modification once construction work was underway. As well as the forts on the actual line of the Wall, there were others to the north (outpost forts) and to the south: the Wall never existed in isolation, but as part of an complex network of forts, camps and other sites, all linked together by the Roman road system, extending throughout northern England and southern Scotland. The study of all this archaeology is a complicated business, about which detailed information is readily available in a variety of publications and at a number of visitor centres, museums and on-site information points throughout the Wall corridor.

Today, nearly two millennia after the Wall's initial construction, its ruins are protected as a World Heritage Site and provide a stunning framework for the Hadrian's Wall Path National Trail. This collection of Graeme Peacock's splendid photographs makes an ideal souvenir for people fortunate enough to have walked all or part of the trail, while also offering a flavour of the Wall and its landscape for those yet to experience Hadrian's Wall Country for themselves.

The western terminus of the Wall was at Bowness-on-Solway *(Maia)*, where today the buried remains of a large fort underlie the village. The church of St. Michael is built largely of stone plundered from the Wall, just one example of the 'recycling' of the Wall in medieval and later times which has left very little of its western third for the modern visitor to see. South-west of Bowness, a system of fortlets, perhaps joined by a timber palisade, extended down the Cumbrian coast past the forts of Beckfoot and Maryport.

Bowness-on-Solway, the western end of Hadrian's Wall.

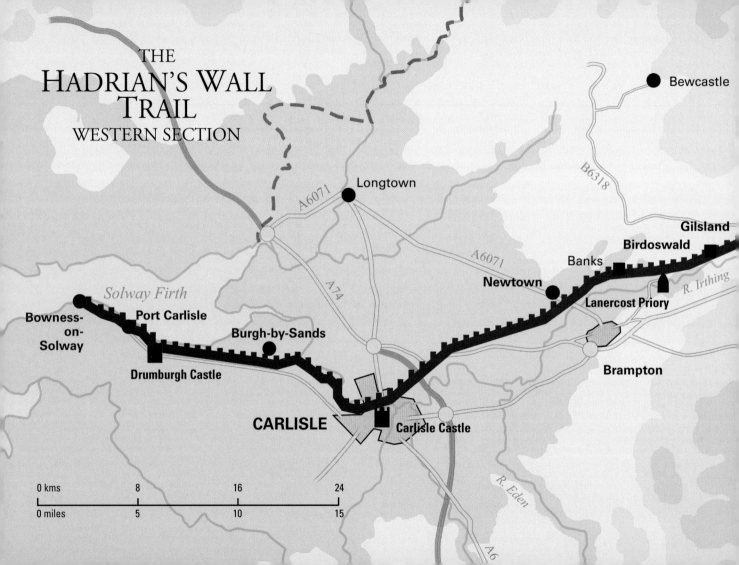

THE
HADRIAN'S WALL
TRAIL
WESTERN SECTION

Bewcastle

Longtown

Solway Firth

A6071

A6071

A74

B6318

Gilsland

Birdoswald

Banks

Newtown

Lanercost Priory

R. Irthing

Bowness-
on-
Solway

Port Carlisle

Burgh-by-Sands

Drumburgh Castle

CARLISLE

Carlisle Castle

Brampton

R. Eden

A6

0 kms	8	16	24
0 miles	5	10	15

Although no longer visible here today, the Wall ran along the southern shore of the Solway, guarding against any attempted sea-borne incursion from the Scottish side. There was a small fort at Drumburgh *(Concavata)*, four miles from the western end of the Wall. This was originally built in turf and timber, and was later rebuilt in stone. Drumburgh Castle, originally an early 14th-century tower but rebuilt as a fortified farmhouse in the early 16th century, incorporates much reused Roman stone, presumably recycled from *Concavata* as well as from the Wall itself.

Above: **Drumburgh Castle, Solway Firth.**
Left: **Walkers at Burgh Marches, Solway Firth.**

Carlisle Castle.

The first Roman fort at the strategic position of Carlisle *(Luguvalium)* was built in AD 72 or 73, when the Romans were moving north in the expectation of conquering Scotland. Half a century later, the largest of all the forts along Hadrian's Wall was built at Stanwix *(Uxelodunum)* opposite Carlisle on the north bank of the Eden. This probably functioned as the headquarters of the entire Wall system, but Carlisle also continued to function in its own right as a military base and civilian settlement. Extensive remains of Roman activity lie buried beneath the streets of the modern city – an essential stopping-off point for anyone touring the Wall. In addition to its splendid cathedral and other historic attractions, visitors must allow time to explore the excellent Tullie House Museum.

Above: **Tullie House, Carlisle.**
Left: **Carlisle Citadel.**

River Eden, Grinsdale, near Carlisle.

Lanercost Priory was founded in about 1166 and survived until the Dissolution of the Monasteries in 1537, when parts of it were converted for domestic use. It has a fascinating history, having played a significant role in medieval Anglo-Scottish border conflict, and still functions as the parish church. Without doubt, it is one of the key 'non-Roman' sites that all Wall tourists should visit. Its fabric includes much stone robbed from the Wall, and its undercroft houses a collection of local Roman and medieval carved stonework.

Although originally linked to Birdoswald fort by a Roman road, Bewcastle *(Fanum Cociddii)* is now rather less accessible. It lies about 10km north of the Wall and is reached via some windy country roads heading into the wild country north of Banks (west of Birdoswald). The peculiar Roman fort here is hexagonal in plan (the vast majority of Roman forts are more-or-less rectangular), but there is little of it to be seen today. However, the fine old church, magnificent stone cross of probable eighth-century date, and medieval castle provide ample reward for those prepared to make the effort to get here.

Above: **Harehill, near Banks.**
Left: **Bewcastle Cross.**

Birdoswald Roman Fort, Gilsland.

Walkers approaching Birdoswald Fort.

One of the most important sites in the history of Wall studies, Birdoswald Fort *(Banna)* saw four major campaigns of excavation between the 1830s and 1990s. Today extensive consolidated remains can be inspected by visitors and the story of the site is presented within a fascinating on-site visitor centre. One of the 'must-see' sites for Wall tourists.

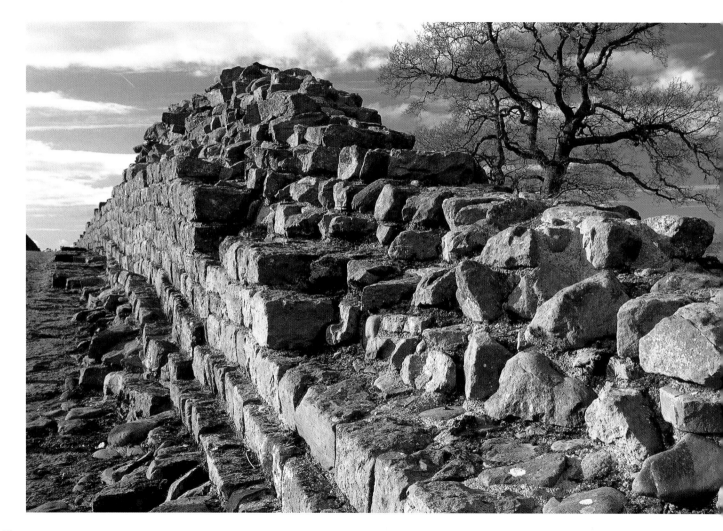

One of the best preserved and most fascinating of the Wall's milecastles can be seen at Poltross Burn, near Gilsland. Visitors can inspect the remains of two barrack blocks (which may have housed a garrison of 32 men) and bread ovens. Nearby, a splendid section of Wall can be seen at Willowford, including the remains of two turrets and an abutment of the Roman bridge over the River Irthing.

*Above: **Poltross Milecastle, Gilsland.***
*Left: **Hadrian's Wall, Willowford, near Gilsland.***

Thirlwall Castle, Greenhead.

Dating originally from the mid 14th century, Thirlwall Castle was built largely from stone plundered from adjacent stretches of Hadrian's Wall. Today, its ruins, recently consolidated and interpreted for visitors, stand as a stark reminder of the turbulent times endured by medieval society in the Anglo-Scottish border zone.

Looking west towards Gilsland from Carvoran.

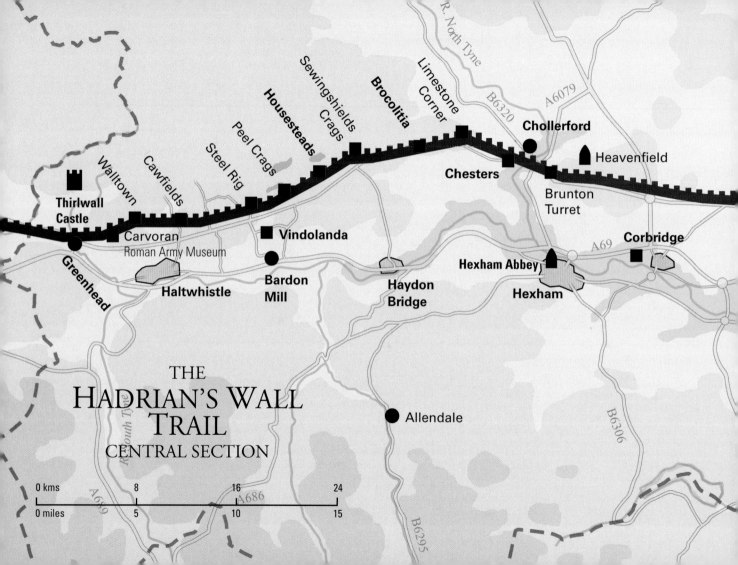

R. North Tyne

B6320

A6079

Limestone
Corner

Sewingshields
Crags

Brocolitia

Housesteads

Chollerford

Peel Crags

Steel Rig

Chesters

Heavenfield

Cawfields

Walltown

Brunton
Turret

**Thirlwall
Castle**

Corbridge

A69

Carvoran
Roman Army Museum

Vindolanda

Hexham Abbey

Greenhead

Haltwhistle

Bardon
Mill

Haydon
Bridge

Hexham

Allendale

THE
HADRIAN'S WALL
TRAIL
CENTRAL SECTION

A689

A686

B6295

B6306

0 kms   8   16   24

0 miles   5   10   15

R. South Tyne

A particularly impressive stretch of the Wall can be followed over Walltown Crags, although this ends rather abruptly at Walltown Quarry where the Wall and the very land it stood on has been quarried away.
Walltown Quarry is now a public open space incorporating a popular geology trail.
Adjacent to the quarry, the Roman Army Museum at Carvoran presents interesting information about the men who built the Wall and served on it.

Above: **Walkers heading west, Walltown.**
Left: **Walltown Crags from the air.**

Walltown Quarry near Greenhead.

In addition to the permanent exhibitions at various points along the Wall, many educational and entertaining events with a Roman theme are held here each year. Demonstrations of Roman military equipment invariably prove popular with visitors of all ages. Details of such events are available from local tourist information offices.

Right: **Standard Bearer.**

Far Right: **Centurion.**

Far Page: **Roman re-enactment, Walltown Crags.**

View east from Cockmount Hill towards Cawfield Crags.

*Left: **Milecastle 42, Cawfields.***

At Cawfields, just as at Walltown, a long stretch of Hadrian's Wall has been quarried away but the old quarry has been landscaped and provides a convenient car park. The remains of Cawfields Milecastle, which overlook the quarry from the east, are well worth visiting. The site perches rather precariously on sloping ground, and any internal buildings here must have been specially designed to stand on the slope. No trace of any such buildings was recorded when the site was excavated in the mid 19th century.

Haltwhistle.

Located at the geographical centre of Britain and just a couple of kilometres south of the Wall, Haltwhistle is a traditional market town offering accommodation and other facilities to Wall tourists.

About a kilometre east of Cawfields Quarry, at a gap through the crags known as Thorny Doors, the Wall still stands fourteen courses high, rising to a height of three metres.
This impressive masonry offers a hint of the awesome nature of the Wall's original appearance.

Left: **Looking west from Thorny Doors.**

The car park at Steel Rigg offers easy access to some splendid walking along the Wall, to the west along Windshields Crags and to the east towards Crag Lough. Just east of the car park, in Peel Gap, a previously unknown tower was discovered when a section of the Wall was excavated in 1986. No doubt the Wall still retains further such secrets, but these will only be revealed when new fieldwork is undertaken.

Left: **Windshields Crags near Haltwhistle.**

Looking east towards Crag Lough, Highshield Crags and Hotbank Crags from above Steel Rig.

Walkers at Steel Rig.

Sycamore Gap achieved international fame when chosen, rather bizarrely, as the location for a scene in the 1991 Film 'Robin Hood – Prince of Thieves', starring Kevin Costner. Many younger visitors now visit this specific spot to have their photograph taken. If nothing else, this site demonstrates that the history of the Wall will never be complete – there is always space for new events to claim a place of their own in the ever-evolving story of the Wall landscape!

*Previous Pages: **Sycamore Gap near Twice Brewed.***
*This Page: **Sycamore Gap in summer and winter.***

Milecastle 39 (Castle Nick) is located in a gap through the crags which may have formed an important routeway for people passing through the Wall: the garrison would have been able to control all such movement. Excavations here uncovered evidence of early timber barracks, later rebuilt in stone, that may have accommodated a garrison of about forty. Fragments of window glass demonstrate that this milecastle had glazed windows for at least part of its life.

View east over Milecastle 39 towards Crag Lough and Highshield Crags.

Looking west over Vindolanda Roman Fort near Bardon Mill.

Thanks to the wonderful work of the Vindolanda Trust over many years, Chesterholm *(Vindolanda)*, located south of the Wall on the Stanegate (the Roman road from Corbridge to Carlisle), is probably the single most fascinating site to visit in the entire Wall corridor. The first fort, of earth and timber, was built here in about AD80, after which the site was continuously occupied through until the fifth century. Visitors can examine the remains of the third/fourth-century stone fort, the extensive civil settlement or vicus, reconstructed sections of Hadrian's Wall and a fabulous museum featuring the incredible Vindolanda writing tablets, along with many other wooden and leather artefacts, which survived here due to the waterlogged nature of certain parts of the site. Visitors may also have the opportunity to inspect excavations in progress, with further exciting finds likely to turn up at any time!

Above:

Top: **Reconstruction of part of Hadrian's Wall.**

Bottom: **Reconstructed Roman temple, Vindolanda.**

Evening light, looking west over Crag Lough and Highshield Crags from Hotbank Crags.

Milecastle 37 is one of the best-preserved milecastles. The massive masonry of the north gate is particularly impressive, although it should be noted that the two highest blocks on both sides had fallen in antiquity and have been replaced in recent times. The remains of a barrack block can be seen within the site, but it is hard to envisage the garrison being kept busy controlling traffic: the north gate opens onto a sheer drop which must have prevented this from being a busy route. The milecastle was presumably built here due to the demand in the Wall blueprint for a milecastle every mile, rather than due to any strategic importance of this particular site.

Milecastle 37 near Bardon Mill.*Milecastle 37 near Bardon Mill.*

In terms of its superb landscape setting and the grandeur of its consolidated remains, Housesteads *(Vercovicium)* is the most visually impressive fort in the Wall corridor: another 'must-see' site on the tourist trail. Alongside the spectacular remains of the fort, which include its four main gates, the commanding officer's house, the headquarters building, the hospital, granaries and barracks, visitors can inspect part of the civilian settlement and an on-site museum. Of particular interest to children are the well-preserved latrines in the south-east corner of the fort.

Above: **Housesteads Roman Fort.**
Left: **Aerial view of Housesteads.**

Looking west over Broomlee Lough from Sewingshields Crag.

The fort of Carrawburgh *(Brocolitia)* was constructed after the Wall had been built, probably in the 130s. There is little here for visitors to see, but the Mithraeum (Temple to Mithras), adjacent to the fort and presumably built by soldiers serving here, is well worth a visit. Mithraism was a popular religion in the Roman army and for a long time rivalled Christianity. This temple seems to have been abandoned during the fourth century, and may have been destroyed by Christians. Just north of the Mithraeum was a shrine to the goddess Coventina, where more than 13,000 coins and many other offerings (some of which can now be seen at Chesters Museum) were deposited in a spring during Roman times.

Above and Right: **Temple of Mithras, Carrowburgh.**

Looking north from Limestone Corner near Walwick.

At Limestone Corner the modern road runs directly on top of the Wall, but the forward ditch (to the north of the Wall) is of interest because the Roman engineers gave up on it – the only place along the entire line where the job was left half-done! Massive blocks of stone, showing chisel marks where the construction gangs had attempted to break them up, still litter the line of the ditch here. It is not known why the ditch was not completed: the usual reason given is that the rock here is unusually hard, but the presence of the vallum ditch in the same rock, just a few metres to the south, demonstrates that this rock could be broken and cleared if necessary. A good section of Wall, along with a turret and the Wall ditch, can be seen east of Limestone Corner at Black Carts.

Aerial view of the vallum, the 'Military Road' and the Wall ditch at Limestone Corner.

Black Carts near Walwick.

Chesters Roman Fort near Chollerford.

In contrast to the wild landscape of the Wall's central sector, Chesters *(Cilurnum)* lies in tranquil parkland adjacent to the North Tyne. It is another key Wall site that all tourists must allow plenty of time to inspect. The remains of several excavated buildings, including the commanding officer's house, the headquarters building and barrack blocks, can be seen within the fort, as can the extraordinarily well-preserved bath-house outside the fort walls. The museum at Chesters houses a wonderful collection of Roman statues, altars and other fascinating objects.

Bath-house, Chesters Fort.

Chollerford Bridge over the North Tyne, Chollerford.

E asily accessible from the adjacent road, the Wall at Brunton Turret still stands six courses high.

The little church of St Oswald sits on the supposed site of the Battle of Heavenfield (634), at which Oswald defeated the pagan Cadwallon thus hastening the acceptance of Christianity throughout Northumbria. The battle was apparently fought adjacent to the crumbling remains of the Wall, abandoned by Rome two centuries earlier.

*Above: **St Oswald's Chapel, Heavenfield near Chollerford.***
*Left: **Brunton Turret, Chollerford.***

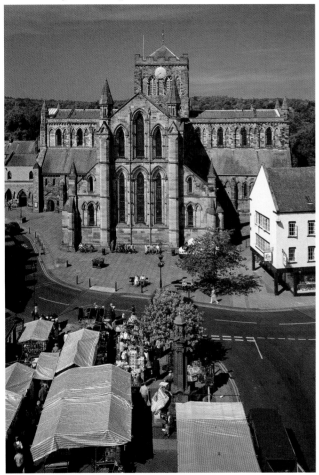

Visitors to Hexham often ask why there are no Roman remains here. The answer is simple: there was nothing of consequence at Hexham prior to the founding of the abbey in the later seventh century. The builders of Hexham Abbey used Roman masonry brought from Corbridge, some of which can still be seen in the crypt.

Corbridge *(Coria or Coriosopitum)* was a key site throughout the Roman occupation, occupying the junction of Dere Street (linking Scotland with York and ultimately London) and the Stanegate which ran west from here to Carlisle. The first fort was built here a year or two before AD80, during the initial Roman campaign into Scotland. The site was later remodelled as a military storage compound and industrial centre, becoming so extensive that many archaeologists refer to it as a town. Visitors can stroll around the remains of several Roman buildings here, and inspect some extraordinary local finds in the on-site museum. It is also well worth visiting St Andrew's Church, the interior of which incorporates a complete arch salvaged from the Roman site.

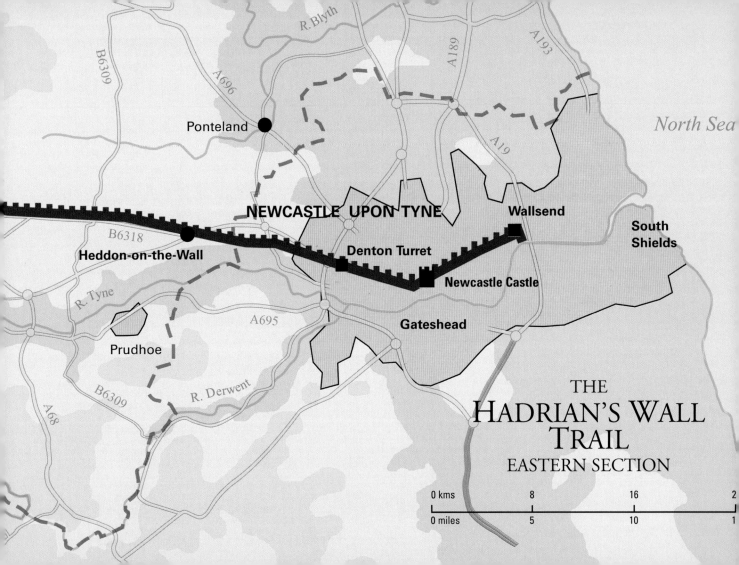

R. Blyth

B6309

A696

A189

A193

North Sea

Ponteland

A19

NEWCASTLE UPON TYNE

Wallsend

B6318

Heddon-on-the-Wall

Denton Turret

South Shields

Newcastle Castle

R. Tyne

A695

Gateshead

Prudhoe

B6309

R. Derwent

A68

THE
HADRIAN'S WALL
TRAIL
EASTERN SECTION

| 0 kms | | 8 | | 16 | | 2 |
| 0 miles | | 5 | | 10 | | 1 |

Between Corbridge and Newcastle the Wall provided a convenient quarry for countless medieval and post-medieval construction projects, and much of it has been lost. However, lengthy but low sections of Wall are easily accessible at Heddon-on-the-Wall (where a potentially confusing circular structure set into the fabric of the Wall is actually a medieval oven or kiln) and Denton Hall, where the remains of a turret can be seen.

*Above: **Denton Hall Turret, Newcastle upon Tyne.***
*Left: **Heddon-on-the-Wall.***

Roman temple, Benwell, Newcastle upon Tyne.

The fort at Benwell *(Condercum)* has been decimated by the construction of a reservoir and housing estate, but the remains of a little temple, surviving incongruously within the housing estate, are worth visiting.

The remains of the Roman fort of Newcastle *(Pons Aelius)* lie buried beneath the heart of the modern city. The name *'Pons Aelius'* means 'Hadrian's Bridge'- the town was named after this bridge which must have been a spectacular structure and may have represented the Wall's original eastern terminus.

Above: **The Millennium Bridge viewed from Gateshead.**
Left: **St Nicholas' Cathedral and the Black Gate, Newcastle upon Tyne.**

*Left: **Remains of Segedunum Roman Fort, Wallsend, from the viewing tower.***

*Above: **Re-enactment at Segedunum Roman Fort.***

Wallsend *(Segedunum)* is marketed as the 'Gateway to the World Heritage Site'. The original eastern terminus of the Wall may well have been at Newcastle, but if so then it was soon extended to Wallsend. Although the site has been much-damaged by industrial activity in recent times, *Segedunum,* with its new visitor centre and impressive 100-feet high viewing tower, along with reconstructions of a bath-house and a length of the Wall, is another 'must-see' site for the Wall tourist.

Arbeia Roman Fort, South Shields.

The Hadrian's Wall Trail, like the Wall itself, ends (or starts) at Wallsend. However, the actual eastern end of the frontier complex lies a little further east at South Shields, where the Roman fort of *Arbeia* overlooks the mouth of the Tyne. Probably founded during Hadrian's reign, *Arbeia* remained in use throughout the occupation, apparently acting for at least part of its life as a supply base for the Wall garrison in addition to its role as a fort. There is much to see here, including excavated remains of the fort and a museum, but it is the recently constructed and hugely impressive full-size replica of the fort's west gate that makes the biggest impression on visitors and propels *Arbeia,* even though it isn't actually on the Wall or the Trail, into the 'must see' category of sites for anyone doing the Hadrian's Wall Trail.